REFLECTIONS
OF MY *Heart*
THROUGH
JESUS CHRIST,
OUR ONLY HOPE

RUTHANN BOND

ISBN 978-1-64191-584-7 (paperback)
ISBN 978-1-64191-654-7 (hardcover)
ISBN 978-1-64191-583-0 (digital)

Christian Faith Publishing, Inc.
832 Park Avenue
Meadville, PA 16335
www.christianfaithpublishing.com

Printed in the United States of America

DEDICATION

I dedicate this book to the One and Only Jesus Christ, my Lord and Savior who rescued me, and I am forever grateful. To my wonderful husband who has been on this journey with me from the start, my biggest fan.

My dear mom who has been such an encourager and kept me on track. My sweet mother-in-law who has always supported me in everything I do. My three amazing children, their spouses, and my ten darling grandchildren who mean everything to me.

The rest of my wonderful family and treasured friends whom I adore.

Thank you. I love you all so much.

7·26·18

To my wonderful neighbors/friends
Dana + Judy,

Jesus is our only hope...

♡ Ruthann

INTRODUCTION

This book of poems is very personal to me. They speak from my heart. Many of them convey a message of either a happy time or a sad time in my life. Some of them I was just trying to get a message out there, but no matter the reason, they all convey that Jesus was in every one of those times.

I never thought that I would publish them. All I wanted was for a poem that I wrote to relate to someone and what they may be going through. Or maybe shine the light and hope of Jesus into their situation. I didn't know I could write. I didn't know that I wanted to write. I came home from work one day back in 2008. All of a sudden, all of these words started coming to me out of nowhere. I went to my desk and started writing them down. It wasn't a long poem, but it was from my heart. I knew it was Jesus giving me the words to express with my pen how my heart was feeling. My Jesus, My Everything is that poem!

Over the past years and currently, an idea will come to me. I will pray and ask the Holy Spirit what he would like to say to people or a specific person in this poem. For you, the reader, I would hope that my words would help to open your eyes and heart to think about life in general and what's important. For you to look at your life, to get real, and to get a fresh, new perspective. You will hear and experience Jesus through my poems. You will experience real life and hope through Jesus Christ.

MY JESUS, MY EVERYTHING

MAY 2008

Each day is a new beginning for me with my Jesus.
A day filled with His mercy, grace, and love for me.
Why is He so wonderful to me?
I definitely do not deserve
what He freely gives me each day.
And why do some of us not accept
this beautiful love that Jesus offers?
We all long for love;
something that can fill the void in our heart.
Why did I refuse this love for so long?
I ask myself, why did I waste so much of my life
searching for a relationship that was calling me
but I ignored?
For now, I know how it feels to be complete
in my Savior, my Redeemer, Jesus Christ;
who has captured my heart forever!

TEARS, MY CLOSEST FRIEND

11.11.11

In the darkness of the night as the tears roll down my face;
they gently place themselves on my pillowcase, as I recall
ever so vividly past days of fear and despair that have now
made their way into my heart again "unaware."
The tears are uncontrollable as they enter the wee hours
of the morning, having to pretend once again that they
never streaked the cheeks on my face as I wash them away.
As we begin another day, my tears, my closest friend,
are waiting to reappear again as the sun fades
and the darkness invades.
You see, that's what gets me through and I look forward to,
as they've become my closest friend.
I haven't meant to, but it seems I've said and done some things,
I wish I could take back.
It's hard being a mom, no matter what the age I've found.
As I love my children, I'm still afraid.
I guess that's just me; need I apologize for that?
As my heart breaks and I don't know what to do,
I hear this still small voice, I am with you.
I've caught every tear and it's good that you cry.
You are human; your heart has a voice that cannot be denied!
I don't know how to be a mom. I think I'm doing right.
Next thing I know I've made a big mess and ask myself why?
I have so many words trapped up inside.
Words that express how I feel about the people in my life.
Words that are dying to be told but can't. Why am I like this, I ask?
They walk out the door; once again the words are trapped,
forever untold.
One day I will regret not having the courage to speak.

I will lie awake all night with tears streaming down my cheeks.
Let's not do that I tell myself. Speak out no matter how it may sound!
Jesus tells me, rest in Me; I try yet struggling.
Deep down, I know He will get me through.
He always does; He always will!
So as the night closes in, my tears will be my closest friend.
Tomorrow will come and the "happy mask" will go on again.
Help me, Lord, through this day. I need you, Jesus,
you are the only way I will get through today!
Maybe tomorrow my tears will fade, but yet I never want to forget,
for my tears have made me who I am today.

ANCHORED IN LOVE

MARCH 27, 2016

The sky grew dark on that dreary day. It was a sad day.
I could see it all.
My emotions scattered like leaves blowing in the wind.
I knew it had to happen, but why?
It had to happen for me. I was the reason. You were the reason.
I thought NO! Why?
LOVE: The love of Jesus, Unconditional love!
As I wept, my hands clasped so tightly,
causing nail marks in my palms.
My heart breaking, saying NO, NO, I'm sorry!
I don't want you to do this for me.
He spoke so gently as He always does, "I have to! I must save you!"
With every lash on His back, I said, "Stay down, stay down!"
So weak yet so strong, He got up. He took more scourging!
I said as I wept, "Stay down, stay down!"
With love, He looked me in the eyes and got back up!
Why would He do that?
He did it so that I could do that! So you could do that!
When we get bulldozed by life's circumstances, we can get back up!
We can keep going!
We can get through and overcome! We can! Jesus did, we can!
He is our refuge! He is our strength! When we are weak, He is strong!
As I recall on that dark, dreary day, with all that He chose to do for
me, I weep again!
I weep with joy! He did it for me! He did it to save me!
He did it for you! He did it to save you!
When I think about the gift of life that Jesus gave me, I smile!
We all believe in miracles. At least we want to!
The miracle of His resurrection was the greatest miracle of all!
Now we can have life, a victorious life!

Easter is not about a bunny! What did a bunny ever do for you?
N-O-T-H-I-N-G!
Let's believe again!
Believe in the One who is the Only way,
the Only truth, the Only life!
Jesus Christ!
The sky grew dark on that dreary day.
My emotions anchored at the foot of the cross!
I raised my hands toward heaven, with tear-stained cheeks.
I said, "Thank You!"
John 3:16

THE SWEETNESS OF HIS GRACE

MAY 29, 2017

God's grace is amazing!
I am so thankful!
Just thinking about it, I find soft,
gentle tears filling my eyes;
such a beautiful emotion.
As I sit here and ponder
thinking about His grace
that fills my life,
never really noticing
the simple yet profound
goodness of His grace.
As He orchestrates, as He shuffles
people and circumstances,
never realizing the abundant love,
the love of Jesus for my heart,
purposing these movements
so that I may live in peace.
God's grace is amazing!
Never intended to be taken advantage of.
Rather to be cherished, treasured, valued,
to be held dearly in every heart.
As God orchestrates our lives,
let us take notice!
He is purposefully allowing things
or not allowing things.
His agenda is such an agenda as to cover us.
To propel us to our destiny
that was designed for us so long ago.

May we long for Him to sear our hearts with His love!
TAKE NOTICE!
Amazing Grace, how Sweet the Sound . . .
My tears, such a beautiful emotion!
May all of our tears be found
in the sweetness of God's grace!

MY NAME IS "HOPE"

JULY 7, 2011

Shhh . .,
Silence swept across the room, the dark room.
It's a secret. No one needs to know . . .
"Hope" is the name I would have chosen.
I bet my hair would have been such a pretty color.
Maybe jet-black and long. I would have liked long hair.
My mommy could have brushed it and made it pretty
while she sang to me. I think hazel eyes with my black
hair would have been so pretty.
Doctor "Hope"! I like it!
If given the chance, I believe I would have chosen to be a doctor.
I could save lives, give people a second chance!
I know that I would have studied real hard.
I would have done my very best.
In doing so, I could have helped a lot of people;
people that were given a chance to live a long, happy life!
Even though I wasn't wanted by my mommy and daddy,
someone might have wanted me.
Maybe this someone was unable to give life, to give a child a chance.
Maybe they would have chosen me?
Every life has value, purpose, destiny.
Why would an adult, who was given life, take mine?
Please don't kill me! Give me a chance!
A chance like your mommy gave you!
A chance to do what I was created to do!
Someone, please help me! I am a person! I have a heartbeat!
I started with a seed, a seed from my mommy and daddy.
Anything that grows must start with a seed, right?
Please listen to me. Please help me.

If someone would save me, I'd like my name to be "Hope."
Hope means promise. Hope means I have a bright future.
I have value, purpose, and destiny!
If my hair isn't black and my eyes are not hazel, that's okay.
I just want to live!
Thank you for saving me! I can grow up and study to be a doctor.
A doctor that will help to save lives. A doctor that will give life!
Thank You for defending me!
Thank You for not staying silent!
Thank You for giving me life!
I have long, jet-black hair. I have beautiful hazel eyes.
I am a doctor. My name is "Hope"

THIS IS MY MOM

JANUARY 28, 2010

When God chose you to be my mom
He knew that He had given me
All that I would need.
So many special qualities
that would nurture me into
whom I have grown to be.
My individuality was put into place
by your uniqueness as a person.
You have always been yourself;
never afraid or intimidated by people or life.
You showed me I could be the same,
by being strong, persistent,
having a great sense of humor, loving life and people.
Being sacrificial, compassionate,
and having a beautiful heart.
I was always inspired and encouraged;
not even knowing.
Such a beautiful individual
filled with passion and love for Jesus.
Your prayers are the most precious gift
you could have ever given me.
The hours you spent on your knees for me,
I will be forever grateful;
for now I have the peace in my heart
that I always longed for.

I feel privileged, thankful, blessed, and chosen
because when God chose you to me my mom,
He knew that He had given me
all that I would need.

Love and Gratitude to you on your eightieth birthday
Your Daughter,
Ruthann Marie

BLESSED TO BE "A MOM"

MAY 11, 2014

As the sun sets, I look back on my day so far; I smile!
Although the sun has set, my day is far from over!
You see, I'M A MOM! That says it all!
Full-time job, for sure, no matter what age your children are.
Changing diapers, taxi service, drying tears, giving hugs
or sleepless nights spent praying with tear-stained pillows.
But truthfully, would we have it any other way?
The joy far outweighs the pain; although I wonder at times.
Let's keep our perspective.
Let's not lose the time we've been given.
C'mon, girls, we need each other!
How 'bout this one? I'm just throwin' it out there.
Grocery stores reveal an unexplainable emotion;
a love-hate relationship; especially for us deli-bakery girls.
Why do I let those magazine covers make me feel so inadequate?
Let's remember, we're the real deal!
Our sweats, T's, hair in a rumble; tells it all!
It's a good thing; the bein' real and all!
You gotta love yourself! You gotta love life!
Your worth, your value is of highest esteem.
Your Heavenly Father knows it. He made you for the world to see!
Be proud of who you are, just the way you are.
Let's work on getting better at some things, God knows I need it!
God made you unique and special in every way.
Young or been around the block a time or two,
(I like that instead of saying old) we have something to say.
Think about your life and who you represent!
Be strong in your faith; let it shine!
Let's show our children the right way to be strong and courageous.

It's NEVER TOO LATE. Let's teach them this.
Have I not commanded you? Be strong and courageous.
Do not be afraid; do not be discouraged,
for the Lord your God will be with you wherever you go.
Joshua 1:9
As I lay my head to rest and I think back on my day,
I pray and thank my Lord Jesus for all my blessings!
I SMILE!

IT IS ME

7.9.13

As the sun wakes up peeking over the mountain,
in the quietness of the morning,
I hear your voice, Lord.
As my troubled mind
tries to influence the events of my day,
I feel your peace, Lord.
As the noisiness of people and things
come rushing in,
I sense your presence, Lord.
The beauty of you, Jesus, overrides all chaos.
If I could only keep my focus on you, I'd be okay.
Teach me to walk in Your light,
Your ways, in the midst of it all.
My selfish flesh creeps in unnoticed
and I seem to give in.
Please help me, Lord!
As worrisome concerns come my way throughout the day,
I call upon your name, Lord.
As I call upon You, Jesus
You beautifully, graciously, and patiently change me.
For it is not the worrisome concerns, chaos, the noise,
or even my troubled mind that is in the way.
It is me!
As I close my eyes at the end of the day, I seek Your peace;
for it is You alone, Lord; only You, Jesus
that opens the eyes of my heart so then I can say yes;

YES to the ONLY ONE who gives me unthinkable
peace that I in my human mind will never understand.
Isn't that what we all truly (if we were really honest) long for?
Peace of mind!
For it is not the worrisome concerns, chaos, the noise,
or even my troubled mind that is in the way.
It is me!

HIS EYES, MY HEART

APRIL 4, 2010

I can't stop thinking about Him; my heart racing.
There He is. I'll never forget his eyes
looking deep into mine, penetrating deep into my soul.
It was like I was transparent.
He could see every addiction, hurt, fear, anxiety, regret, sadness, tear;
down to the loneliest part of me.
Yet at the same time, He could see who He created me to be.
At that moment, it was as if I was the only one.
He spoke these words that I will never forget.
"I MAKE ALL THINGS NEW"
What did He mean? What is He telling me?
I began thinking about what "NEW" means to me.
Spotless, flawless, no defects, sparkles, clean,
refreshing, and irresistible.
Suddenly I realized that what "NEW" meant to me,
Is what "HE IS"
I now know what He was telling me; what He meant.
Only in Him I can be made new.
All the transparency, of my heart and soul,
past and present can be made new.
He did this for me and for you.
He willingly went to the cross and died.
Everything we need starts at the cross;
The cross that represents love and healing.
How did I not see this?
This undeniable sacrifice.
This love beyond human comprehension.
My heart breaking with every thought of Him.

I love Him! I believe in Him!
How can I not, when He died for me.
He looked deeply into my eyes;
penetrating deep into my soul.
He told me, I will make you new.
I will heal all the broken places of your heart.
You will be who I created you to be.
I will never forget those beautiful, tender eyes
that spoke so much love into my heart.
As my heart races to the cross for everything I need,
I will love my Jesus forever!
For this is who "HE IS"

I WAS MADE FOR YOU

JULY 19, 2009

The Creator of all! So majestic yet gentle.
So mighty yet personable. Full of justice yet merciful.
How can we comprehend such differences,
but yet sense His presence?
We were made in His image!
In His wonderful, creative way,
He intended for One Man and One Woman
to be joined together in marriage!
Knowing from the beginning that they would have their differences,
but always promising to be with them through it all!
Hang on to the most precious relationship(s) you have;
Jesus Christ and the one and only husband or wife!
Cling to the ones so precious, so few.
Know deep in your heart the choice you made
is right in every way!
Relax and enjoy the ride!
For deep down, you know that Jesus is on your side!

MY SPECIAL-ORDER DAD

JUNE 20, 2010

Sometimes, I just sit and wonder about stuff.
You know, like what would it be like
if I had a different house or lived in a different state.
Or what if I had little dogs instead of big dogs.
How about if I didn't have a house or family at all
and just lived wherever.
That's sad to me when I think about that.
But there's a lot of people like that,
and I wish I could help all of them.
Sometimes, I think about how I take things for granted,
like everything I do have and even my family.
I wish I could change that and I will.
And you know what else?
Sometimes I wonder if I could have "special-ordered" my dad,
how would I have placed that order.
Something like this I think:

1. Any size or shape, I'm not picky.
2. He loves me all the time even when I'm not so good.
3. I can talk to him about anything and he just listens.
4. He takes time to spend just with me.
5. He's fun to be around and play with.
6. He lets my friends come over anytime.
7. He can do anything; he's my hero.
8. He loves my mom and treats her
    with kindness and kind words.
9. Honesty and integrity are written all over him.
10. He teaches me by example.
11. He loves Jesus and teaches me about Him.

You see, I don't need a dad who's rich or famous or even perfect.
I just need a dad who is present and makes me feel wanted and special.
Guess what? My order is placed!
"My dad" is exactly the dad I ordered!
Maybe he needs to work on some things, but I'll help him.
We'll do it together.
I've kinda had a chance to think about things.
I don't want to take anything for granted anymore,
especially my family!
I need my family, especially my dad!
Dad, please teach me about Jesus. I want to know Him.
I know He made you and me for each other.
Can you please show me how to thank Him?
I love you, Dad. I'm so glad you're my dad!
My special-order dad; he's my hero!

THE FORGOTTEN HOLIDAY

NOVEMBER 24, 2011

The hype of Christmas is in the air.
That's all you see everywhere!
It's only October with temps in the 90s,
yet we see the red, the green, the ribbons, the trees!
Our mailboxes cluttered with catalogs galore;
where are my bills? oh who cares anymore!
Hurry, the weekend sales are starting without us.
Money spent now, money spent then,
'cause were all caught up in the glitter,
lights, and all that hype!
Wait! Wait! November is here! Fall is in the air.
My mind now transfers into the present.
Into the present; my heart reminding me,
It's the month for "THANKSGIVING"!
Shouldn't it be an all-year thing?
But how can it be when I'm caught up in all
those other material things!
It should have my full attention; oh now I see!
It's become "THE FORGOTTEN HOLIDAY"!
All wrapped around the turkey, the trimmings—
NAPTIME ANYONE!
Hmmm, how did this food get here?
Who are you sitting across from me?
With a roof over our heads, our warm cozy beds,
clothes to wear and shoes on our feet.
Shouldn't we forget for a while
all the petty aggravations, mistakes we have made.
Maybe we should say
"THANK YOU," Heavenly Father for my family!

Think of others besides yourself.
Give to the homeless, orphans, widows, and the poor.
Wake us up, Lord Jesus, give us your heart!
We can be so selfish. Sit in our own self-pity.
We have so much to be thankful for!
"THE FORGOTTEN HOLIDAY," how sad is that.
Our opportunity is now; let's make a change.
Let's all come together and say,
"THANK YOU,"
Lord, for everything!
I am grateful to you! I am grateful for you!
What are you thankful for? Give it some thought.
This year, let's put "THANKSGIVING" in her rightful spot!

THE WARZONE WITHIN

JULY 27, 2011

A rush through my head like an exploding bullet.
A knife through my heart that should have killed me.
The words that pierced my soul that I will never forget.
The heartache so deep inside of me; when will it go away?
Who will help me? I'm stuck in this ocean of despair.
For how long I ask?
The longing that I feel in my heart cries out for peace.
Oh, restless heart, how do I find the companion
that can relieve the emptiness
that tortures me all night long?
Oh, God of heaven, can you hear my cry?
I cry out to you, for I know deep, deep down in my brokenness,
you aren't afraid to walk into my warzone.
Within me, there is a battle, a battle for my life.
But you, oh God, will fight for me until the end!
I am living a slow death; I need life again!
How do I finally surrender?
I've lived in this warzone, it seems, all of my life!
Help me, Jesus! I can't do it alone anymore!
I scream now for help! I can't live in this warzone any longer!
My flesh won't admit it, but my heart does!
Jesus, my warrior, please come to my rescue!
A rush through my head like grace so amazing!
A knife through my heart, capturing every part of it!
The words that pierced my soul, graciously, with such love!
My heartache transformed into joy!
When I think about my past with the warzone within,
it brings me to my future.
You see, my past is the place I used to live.

I need my past to get me to my future!
PAST+PRESENT+FUTURE = JESUS WITHIN
My warzone is now my peace zone!
Today, this is where I live!
And I know that you, O God,
will fight for me until the end!

"REMEMBER WHEN"

SEPTEMBER 11, 2011

Thoughts of yesterday are like beautiful wildflowers dancing
in the breeze of a cool autumn day;
bringing back memories of our yesterdays.
From the very first day of life, memories begin.
So many memories that many of them we will forget.
Maybe because they were memories that did not impact our life in a
significant way or they were hurtful and we choose to forget!
Why are memories important to us?
I believe memories are our pathway to bringing our past
together with our present and future days.
To believe that when we are remembering,
no matter what feelings and emotions those memories may bring,
they are helping us to build our character of
integrity, compassion, empathy, truth, and love!
Unfortunately for some, it may be burying hurt,
harboring hate, resentment, bitterness, and unforgiveness.
An explosion of life unfolds as suddenly as a lightning strike,
leaving you with uncertainty, unanswered questions!
With that uncertainty, with those unanswered questions,
brings your response, your perception of that explosion.
The interruption of life invades your whole being.
You ask the question WHY? Why me? Why now or why ever?
Time; those yesterdays; those memories flash before you
like a sweet fragrance reminding you
of why they are important to you!
Why you must hold on to them! Why you must cherish them!
Why you must not take them for granted!
We must believe that our days are numbered,
that our lives are but a vapor.

We must be ready, keep that firm foundation
which can only be found in Jesus Christ!
When we live in those uncertain times,
when we have those unanswered questions,
that's when we can go back, remember when, recall the strength
from the character we have built through the years.
Our character is strong; filled with
integrity, compassion, empathy, truth, and love!
We refused to let the others take root and destroy!
We are now able to help others navigate
the same path we have been down.
Together, we travel this road of life!
This life of daily being ready to meet our Maker!
The one who truly will comfort and heal our broken hearts!
The one who has made it possible for us to pause and to be calm.
I want you to take yourself back to those thoughts of yesterday.
Close your eyes; watch the beautiful wildflowers
dance in the breeze of that cool autumn day.
Let the tears freely fall as you "REMEMBER WHEN"

LOVE IS CHRISTMAS

DECEMBER 25, 2014

I sit at my desk as I have many times before.
This time is different.
I sit here with my eyes closed; my emotions overwhelm me
as I experience all over again anew,
the love of Jesus inside of my heart.
My heart longs for you to experience the love of God!
Experience it all over again anew! Experience it for the very first time!
Experiencing the love of God is really ALL that matters!
NOTHING ELSE MATTERS!
When you experience the love of God,
your whole outlook on life changes.
Life can be a twisting, turning, rocky road at times!
Your outlook during those times is what makes the difference!
We say, "There's just something about the Christmas season.
OR Christmas is in the air."
IT'S JESUS! There's NO OTHER REASON!
Take Jesus out and you have NOTHING!
A bunch of presents that can be wiped out in an instant.
A bank account that's empty!
CHRISTMAS IS JESUS! That's why we feel like we feel.
That's why we get all emotional! Don't you get it?
It's the love of God through His son Jesus Christ! It's wonderful!
Why we fight the truth I will never understand.
Experience the love of God. You will NEVER be the same!
Inside of me is an explosion of love, laughter, joy, and peace.
You know why? The love of Jesus lives in my heart!
One day 15 years ago, I wept as I prayed:
Dear Jesus,
I need a change in my life. I need you to come and live in my heart.

I ask you to please forgive me of my sins. I believe in you
that you are the Son of God.
Fill me with life again. Fill me with your love.
Thank You, Jesus. Amen.
As I sit here in awe of my Lord and what He has done for me,
I weep with great gratitude.
I am overwhelmed by His love for me. He loves you the same.
Christmas is Jesus! That's why we feel like we feel
the excitement; the anticipation!
He is why we get all emotional. His love is trying to get in!
Open your heart and let Jesus in! HE LOVES YOU!

THIS YOUNG MAN

MAY 9, 2009

I once knew a young child so fragile, so dependent.
Becoming a young boy with gorgeous, golden, flowing hair.
Full of life, courageous, and spirited!
All of a sudden, a young man
that I didn't recognize anymore,
although I tried.
Full of such potential and promise.
Every day my heart full of faith, tears, joy, sadness,
peace, weariness, knowing, but most of all grace!
Never giving up, never giving in! Fighting for this young man!
Suddenly one day, this young man became someone
that in the deepest part of me I knew he would become.
The wait was hard but the worth, priceless!
FAITH: being sure of the things we hope for and knowing
that something is real even if we do not see it.
I love this young man with all my heart!
He is handsome, kind, loving, and smart with a
compassionate, generous spirit.
Still full of life, courageous, and spirited!
What a joy he is in my life!
This young man is my son, and I am his mom.

THIS MOM'S PRAYER
FOR MY SON

APRIL 15, 2014

How precious the moments as I held you in my arms.
Words will never be able to describe my love for you.
A Mother and her Son, such a unique and special bond that no one
could ever break or separate. The tenderness of hearts as they collide!
Dear Lord,
As I will never be able to put into words
what I am feeling, the beating of my heart begs for your ear.
Although I never dreamed I'd be where I am today,
as I look at all the portraits on the wall; I am here.
Yet no matter what, my love grows more endearing, ever stronger.
I pray to You as if the words will never end;
as the tears make a pillow for my head to rest.
Protect him, cover him, care for him, change him, renew, restore,
refresh, revive him, comfort him, give him peace, may he know how
much You love him and have wonderful plans for him.
That You will never give up on him and neither will I!
My prayer of tears my Lord hears, even more than words.
As I stare at this paper, I relive many tender memories;
my heart has a collection of them all.
I picture his handsome face, his beautiful smile, as I have not seen him
in a while. But I know You are with him, Lord, as You are with me,
filling that void of loneliness, the missing of our times together.
They will be again; Your faithfulness never ends!
And, Lord, thank you that the dreams and desires of my son's heart
will come true as You have heard the cry of his heart.
As they are his cry, so they are mine.

This mom knows that she can trust You Lord as You want the very best for my son. I give him to You and ask You to draw us together although we are apart. How precious are the moments, son, as I hold you in my heart!
Thank You, Lord, for listening to every teardrop
as the stain will forever be
an impression of two hearts:
MOM and SON

WHY TRUTH?

APRIL 20, 2014

TRUTH—
What Is TRUTH?
Have we lost its meaning?
In a world with compromise and little white lies.
Webster says truth is:
The real state of things; fact or actuality; correctness. Honesty.
This is what the Bible says, John 14:6
Jesus said, "I am The Way, The TRUTH, and The Life."
Who stands up for truth? Do I? Do You?
Truth gives us peace! Truth gives us joy!
All day, every day, no matter what it may look like.
Truth lets us sleep at night!
Like a winding road going nowhere. Like a tornado
spinning out of control,
or a book full of suspense and anxiety.
Maybe even a patch of black ice that's invisible, unnoticed,
yet capable of taking us to a place we'd rather not be.
A place of feeling lost, alone, and afraid.
This is real; feeling like there's no way out;
stuck in the quicksand of life!
Decide now that you're not staying there! Decide now, with me!
The TRUTH is so beautiful, so simple, yet we make it so difficult!
Jesus came, died, and rose again to give us LIFE! To give us TRUTH!
ASK! BELIEVE! DECIDE! Only YOU can decide!
The Gospel Message is so beautiful, so simple,
yet we make it so difficult!
THIS IS TRUTH
Psalm 121:1, 2
I lift my eyes unto the hills. Where does my help come from?

My help comes from the Lord; The Maker of Heaven and Earth.
Truth is what we long for! Truth is what we need!
This is what the Bible says
John 14:6
Jesus said, "I am The Way, The TRUTH and The Life."
Jesus also said in John 8:32,
"And you will know The TRUTH and The TRUTH
will set you free."
Who stands up for truth? Do I? Do you?
JESUS CHRIST IS TRUTH! JESUS CHRIST IS LOVE!
ASK! BELIEVE! DECIDE TODAY!
Our lives are but a vapor.
Here today, gone tomorrow. James 4:14

UNFORGETTABLE YOU!

{A LOVE STORY}
MAY 27, 2010

They say "Love is a Wonderful Thing." But is it really?
How can it be, when the meaning of love has been so misunderstood;
the word itself, so misused! Love is an experience!
You have to experience love to know what it is right?
I've heard it said that there's one "true love" for everyone.
But it's such a sad thought to know that many hearts
walking around have never experienced true love,
found that "one" that's just right for them.
That special look, an inviting touch, a warm feeling,
a closeness that brings security.
Wanting to be wanted by someone. And in some hearts, anyone.
I LOVE YOU! Who said that?
That voice had such tenderness and genuineness flowing from it.
What was that? I've never felt a touch like that, so gentle, so tender.
Is that what it feels like? My heart beating anxiously
as I recall that voice, that touch.
It was as if this person that spoke to me, that touched me,
loves me for me; for who I am right this moment.
I don't have to pretend to be someone else.
I don't have to try to impress or prove anything.
He was just here. He came to me. He said,
"I Love You"; He touched me.
Do you know how long I've desired in my heart for this kind of love?
When I least expected it, in a mysterious way,
love showed up in my world.
This love that is saying to my heart; I Love You.
I Adore You. I Appreciate You.
I Need You. I will NEVER give up on You!

Then He spoke deeply into my heart, saying:
You are a portrait of beauty in my eyes. I can't take my eyes off you.
I can't get you off my mind. You are unforgettable,
the apple of my eye.
Do you know this One who has loved you all along?
The moment you were conceived, from the moment
you came into existence.
Even before time, I created you so I could love you.
I AM LOVE! Come, experience it with me.
You know me, but I want you to know me in a much deeper way!
I want us to be inseparable! I love you this much!
I long for the love between us to be a "true love" experience; a
"Wonderful Thing."
Follow Me closely! Don't let go of My hand!
You are so precious in My sight. You are wanted and needed.
You are a flawless diamond in the Kingdom of My Father.
My Father asked me to come to you.
He wants you to know He needs you; He has so much for you!
Keep looking, keep expecting, keep growing!
He wants you to know you are truly irreplaceable, truly unforgettable!
Keep Me close to your heart.
I am the One who touched you. I am the One who said,
"I Love You."
I AM JESUS, AND THIS IS THE BEGINNING OF
"OUR" LOVE STORY.

INFLUENCIAL DADS

(THAT'S YOU)
JUNE 16, 2013

As for me and my house, we will serve the Lord!
Should there be any other way?
I love you, Daddy, coming from that sweet, innocent voice!
Those gentle words piercing through your heart!
How precious these days of youth!
What a privilege to be a dad!
The provider, the protector, the priest,
the lover of your family, your home.
Come play with me, Daddy.
To be wanted. What a wonderful experience.
Help me, Lord, to give all that I have.
To be the Dad you called me to be.
To influence my children in such a way
that they follow YOU all of their days!
I love you, Dad! Can we spend some time together?
I will cherish those words; they will never fade.
The responsibility; do not take it for granted.
To be a dad, what a precious gift from God.
Dad, will you teach me how to drive?
How I will treasure these times together that will not last forever.
Lord, please give me patience and love through these trying years.
Help me to teach and to understand.
I'm going away, Dad. I will miss our times together!
WHAT JUST HAPPENED?
The overwhelming emotion in your heart is almost
more than you could bear!

The expressions of your heart must always be shared.
I will cling to the memories and never let them go.
I am the provider, the protector, the priest,
the lover of my family, my home!
Thank you for everything, Dad!
I LOVE YOU!

MY HEROES

MAY 12, 2013

As I sit, as I think, as I wonder,
I'm thinking about all of you.
All of you moms!
What do I say to you?
How do I express to you what you "stamp" on this world!
How you impact your children, grandchildren.
You are beautiful, lovely, strong, and courageous.
Your smile reflects the sun as it rests upon the meadow.
You are teachers, counselors, nurses, and peacemakers.
You can endure, persevere through the toughest of times!
You are angels in disguise. You are heroes in my eyes!
Our Father in heaven has blessed you.
He downloaded into you the will to fight, to defend.
He favored you with character, a sense of humor!
(thank you, Jesus, 'cause I need that if you're in my family!)
You know, uh huh!
Your Father in heaven adores you. He honors you.
He smiles when He looks at you.
His eyes well up with tears
when you come to Him,
with yours!
He catches every one, turning them into a beautiful rose!
You have such style and flair that belongs to only YOU!
I admire your tenderness, your compassion.
Your heart is adorned with grace;
the love you illuminate is contagious!

Your presence instills security,
bringing confidence to all those around you.
As I sit, as I wonder, as I write,
my heart is filled with emotion for you.
You touch my life more than you know!
You are angels in disguise. You are heroes in my eyes!

WHAT SHE'S BECOME

9.20.08

How can this be?
Who do I see standing beside me?
Am I imagining it? Is it a dream?
How did this happen?
Time passed in front of me so quickly.
For now beside me she stands;
a portrait of beauty, elegance, and grace.
A flower that has come into full bloom;
now bringing me my little blossom to cherish, to love.
Watching her beautiful qualities unfold into this life
she is bringing into her world of security, laughter,
unmeasurable love and faith in Jesus Christ, our Sweet Savior.
Next to me is my lifetime of blessing; my dream come true.
My beautiful daughter, standing beside me.

THREE ANGELS

APRIL 14, 2012

Have you ever seen angels from heaven?
Jesus blessed me with three!
They are on loan from Him so I can see
His gift of love He has for me.
To me, they are my grandchildren
with such meaningful names as these.
Lily, Tyson, and Dominic, full of promised destiny!
The times we spend together are priceless but few.
I can't tell you how I long in my heart
to be with them when time allows me to.
Deep down inside, I know that being a Grammie
is a special season in my life.
I wouldn't trade it for anything; it's like sugar and spice!
So hugs and kisses I will give them every chance I get.
Lily, Tyson, and Dominic are precious gifts from God
that I will treasure, that I will keep in my heart.
Forever and always, we will never part
for my Jesus will always protect them as He has from their start.
Have you ever seen angels from heaven?
You think you haven't, you better look all around.
I guarantee, they will appear,
maybe even in your own stomping ground!
I won't take them for granted.
I'll hold them close to my heart.
I will pray for them to live for Jesus, knowing their future
is destined to be a priceless work of art!
My three angels, our hearts entwined.
With Jesus in our circle, we are of one mind.
My three angels full of promised destiny,
will give me joy forever
because in Jesus, they will live in perfect harmony!

BRAYDON IS MY NAME

AUGUST 10, 2013

I can see you! PEEK-A-BOO!
My heart and your heart bouncing off each other in joyous applause!
MY LIFE HAS BEGUN—
Understand, my life began at conception!
My Daddy and Mommy want me! I was created in love!
I am a human being. From the very beginning,
life was breathed into me.
My journey has been filled with such wonder
as I will continue to grow.
To realize the truth, the truth about my life, why I am being created!
I LOVE MY MOMMY!
I know sometimes with her helping me grow,
she gets tired and her legs hurt.
THANK YOU, MOMMY! I know you love me!
My Daddy, I know he loves me!
He touches my mommy's tummy so gently and talks to me.
He tells me, I AM SPECIAL!
I can hear my big brother playing.
He's getting all of our toys ready so we can play together.
HE'S MY TYSON, MY BEST FRIEND!
I can sense, as my big sister is anticipating my debut!
She will hold me. She will tell me stories.
She will teach me to lead, not follow!
SHE'S MY BIG SISTER, MY LILY!
My mommy adores me as she gives me good food
that keeps me strong.
I'm so glad my mommy cheats too but only once in a while.
Then I get that sweetness that only comes from her!
I feel you! TICKLE, TICKLE!
I'm giving you a BIG hug, my family that is only mine!

As I flip, stretch, turn, and hiccup,
I remind you, I AM HERE!
Do you see me in my picture?
I grasp every moment, as God intricately and carefully
puts me into motion; forming me inside my mommy!
You know my name is BRAYDON!
I am strong in mind, body and spirit!
I have been made to touch your life in a very special way!
All babies are made to do that, you know!
PEEK-A-BOO! I can almost see you.
As my heart leaps with excitement. I am almost ready.
Ready to enter into this beautiful life that is only mine,
but to share with you!
Influence me with GOOD THINGS!
I will analyze, understand, and learn.
I WILL MAKE A CHANGE! I HAVE BEEN GIVEN LIFE!
I HAVE BEEN CHOSEN!
BRAYDON IS MY NAME!

RECEIVE THE GIFT

DECEMBER 25, 2010

Christmas! What does it mean to you? Why do we give presents?
Why do we celebrate on December 25?
And why are most people so giving,
caring, and loving during this season more than any other?
Christmas is magical! It gives you a feeling that's indescribable.
For me, Christmas fills me with many emotions.
Sometimes, I cry when I hear Christmas songs.
I smile when I see the faces of innocent children.
I adore the elderly with so much wisdom.
And for the rest of us, I wish we would learn from both.
All the colors of the Christmas lights announcing their presence.
Such beautiful arrangements dancing on our homes,
streets, and churches.
In our homes, our Christmas trees expressing our own uniqueness.
Even now, the emotion that I feel in my heart is breaking
for those that are sad,
lonely, and have no reason to celebrate.
They have no hope.
Sometimes, I feel lonely. You may admit the same,
but only to yourself.
Sometimes I feel alone, and I cry.
One day I was talking to Jesus, you know he does listen.
I told him that sometimes I am lonely,
even though I'm with people and in a crowd.
My heart misses my family. I think this may be a good kind of lonely.
It's a good thing that I miss my family.
That means I care about them and love them.
Maybe we all need to be lonely in this way and cry.
Jesus cries because he's lonely. Lonely for you!

He misses you! He cares for you! He loves you!
Jesus has real feelings like you and I.
Right now, he is hurting in his heart. He longs for you
to be a part of his family.
He's waiting! He's waiting for you to say yes to him.
He's coming again this December 25 to tell you he loves you.
He came for you.
Christmas is beautiful, it's magical! It's caring, sharing,
and loving people.
There's just something about it. I believe that
"something" that we feel;
that special emotion that we cannot explain
or put into words is JESUS!
He can do that to your heart.
His love is amazingly powerful. Don't ignore
the true meaning of Christmas any longer.
Listen to what your heart is telling you. You hear it, don't you?
Jesus wants this Christmas to be your best Christmas ever!
He wants you to celebrate with gifts, music, and lights.
He takes pleasure in watching you enjoy these.
He wants you to enjoy them.
Just keep in mind in all the crazy, busy stuff,
that you need to be sure that this Christmas
is the one you will never forget.

You will always remember it because for the first time you will celebrate the true meaning of Christmas.

Jesus won't be lonely anymore. He'll have you! He'll cry happy tears!

I want to give you the message of "HOPE" this Christmas.

This year may you rediscover again, or for the first time,

the true meaning of Christmas!

Receive Jesus

Receive the Gift

The Best Gift of All!

THE "RIGHT" CHOICE

APRIL 8, 2012

What's happened to our world? What's happened to the people in it?
I can do what I want, when I want, how I want! If it feels good, do it!
Just go with the flow! Whatever works for you!
Selfishness, No Respect for others, Rude Gestures!
It's okay, as long as it doesn't hurt anyone?
Oh, but it does; it hurts YOU!
Do we not stand up for what is morally right anymore?
Do we even know what "Morality" means?
Where is our courage? Have we just accepted it?
Please tell me NO! Have we become complacent, comfortable?
It's easy to just "Go with the flow."
It's easy to "Do what I want, when I want, how I want"
FORGIVENESS!
We all need it, don't we? I need it every day!
What about working for what is right?
Who wants to work anymore? Let's play; let's have things easy!
What has happened to us?
MORALITY: The quality of being in accord
with standards of right or good conduct.
Virtuous conduct; having moral excellence; admirable.
Working for what is morally right takes our time.
It takes sacrifice, determination, courage, and love! IT'S A CHOICE!
That's what Jesus did for us! He did what was right. He had a choice.
He could have told his Father "NO"! But did he? No, he didn't!
He didn't take the easy way out; He couldn't!
He cared for us, for our future. He loved us!
His heart so heavy with our sin, His creation that He loved,
His creation that He adored!
He had to do something drastic! Something that took
His time, His sacrifice,

His determination, His courage, and His love!
HE WENT TO THE CROSS!
Are we thankful? Look at us! How thankful we all
should be that He did!
For now the same hands that were nailed to that cross,
that bled for me,
are the same hands that touch me, heal the broken places
of my life, and make me whole.
Those same hands wipe the tears that stream down my face
and hold me when I am lonely.
How I will treasure forever in my heart those hands that replaced mine!
As tears of joy gently travel ever so tenderly
landing on my heart, I will forever
love the man that took the nails for me! Jesus captured
my heart with His love for me.
He tugged at my heartstrings with every excruciating lash He endured!
What I want to do now is love Him back, live for Him!
It's the least I can do.
Take a stand, be bold, sacrifice your time,
be determined in your mind, be courageous,
love the unlovely; the hurting, for all of us are unlovely;
we hurt too until we let Jesus in.
For now is the time to do what is right. For now is the time
to fight the moral fight.
For if not now, when? Now is the time to make The "Right" Choice.
As tears of love gently stream down my Savior's face,
He quietly calls your name to say,
"I LOVE YOU!"
He went willingly to the cross for you! His hands replaced yours!
Now the "CHOICE" is yours!

MY TWO WORLDS

MAY 29, 2017

My past haunts me again,
like an eerie light off in the distance.
My emotions revealing something so sweet
as if I was walking through
a garden of mixed fragrances.
At times, my two worlds clash! I'm forced to pick one.
The one I choose is out of duty, out of responsibility.
My heart wants to run; my heart wants to chase,
but it is stopped by its own call to finish what it started.
LOYALTY: dedication, devotion, fidelity, faithfulness.
I was awakened as my past called out to me;
wanting me to come to it.
I fought hard trying to forget but yet longing to remember.
Maybe my tears will wipe it away, but only until it reappears
unexpectedly as it did tonight.
I will hide; I will go on as if my past never existed.
I must secretly live in my own pain of choices.
It's okay. I've had many years of practice.
I hide it well beneath layers of heartache and regret.
At times, my two worlds clash!
As I wash my tears, it's my secret.
I will fall back asleep now as if these emotions never happened.
Everything will be buried again!

YOU-NIQUELY CREATED

9/18/14

You made all the delicate, inner parts of my body and knit me together in my mother's womb. Thank you for making me so wonderfully complex! Your workmanship is marvelous and how well I know it. You watched me as I was being formed in utter seclusion, as I was woven together in the dark of the womb. You saw me before I was born. Every day of my life was recorded in your book.
EVERY MOMENT WAS LAID OUT
BEFORE A SINGLE DAY HAD PASSED.
Psalm 139:13–16
LIFE: what an amazing yet interesting journey!
Each journey is designed especially for each of us.
The path that we travel can be filled with
unexpected adventure, allowing our faith and character
to grow, progressively building stronger, bolder!
True beauty for the onlooker is seeing the strength
and the confidence in the life that is soaring
up and down while traveling the path of unexpected
adventure; steadily, gracefully displaying
the beauty of God's love and faithfulness!
You were chosen for this specific journey;
the journey to inspire, to bring hope,
to offer wisdom; wisdom that speaks
DO NOT TAKE YOUR LIFE AND WHAT YOU WERE
CREATED TO DO FOR GRANTED!
You were You-niquely Created!
You were born to display the courage to conquer fear.
Your journey is yours alone. No one can take it from you!
Unfolding in your journey is the beauty
of God's love and faithfulness, sheltering you
in the secret place of the Most High!

LIFE, with all of its twists, turns, ups, downs,
mountains, valleys, and unexpected adventure;
Would you want it any different?
As you allow your faith and character to grow and build,
through the hard times, the difficult times,
the uncomfortable times, you will become
that individual that God chose to thrust
into your intended purpose!
As you consider
"EVERY MOMENT WAS LAID OUT
BEFORE A SINGLE DAY HAD PASSED,"
Believe by faith that you can rest in the arms of Jesus!
He is faithful and true! YOU ARE SAFE! Trust and Believe!
YOU-NIQUELY CREATED, THAT'S YOU!

PRICELESS

JUNE 20, 2010

What can this be compared to? Anything?
Can a price be put on it?
Something so precious and immeasurable.
Something, that no matter what the age,
a child's heart deeply longs for.
What could this be?
This thing that is so often not shown or said.
But most importantly the sound
that is missing from a relationship.
Could it possibly be the love that only
a father can show, genuine love.
Love that means many things to a child.
Not only by saying it, but by showing it.
There is only one chance at this,
and it passes oh so quickly.
Tell them every day. Show them every day.
Don't let another day go by
without doing this patiently and tenderly.
Love the Lord your God
With all your heart, soul, mind, and strength.
Then this thing that will never have a price tag,
but if given unconditionally, will have
a lifetime of no regrets.
A lifetime of endless, unforgettable memories.
A Father's love, Priceless!

WHO IS THIS MAN

APRIL 27, 2010

Have you ever wondered why God gave the gift
of a certain individual to you?
An individual with so many special qualities,
with so much to offer.
Someone that would so generously pass down to you
life lessons, so that possibly one day, you could be
that same gift to someone else.
I often sit under the noonday sun or maybe
stare into the whisper of the night or even while I'm
enjoying the freshness of the morning;
I recall many special moments.
Moments that could not have been
given to me by anyone else.
I drift away into a place that was ours alone.
A place of security.
A place of never forgetting what only he could teach.
A place of laughter and happy times.
A place of longing in my heart,
for his warm, inviting touch.
Handsome, oh yes!
Sense of humor, of course!
An encourager and an inspiration like no other!
Unconditional love like I've never seen!
I think I will look back now, and in my heart,
relive the many special moments
that I had with this gift,
that was given to me by God.
This gift has a name;
and to me he was my dad.

LOVELY THOUGHTS OF YOU, GOD'S CREATIONS

MAY 10, 2015

LOVED
A kiss on the cheek from your child who strayed but has come home, always believed.
VALUED
A walk on the beach barefoot, feeling the sand squeeze between your toes; I'm ME.
COVERED by GOD'S GRACE
A cool breeze wisping through your hair, falling as it may, always knowing.
BLESSED
A refreshing glass of strawberry lemonade on a hot summer day, never taken for granted.
STRONG
Memories of that special loved one that will always bring a tear with a smile.
UNIQUE
As every star twinkles in the night, spelling out your name.
BEAUTIFUL
Twelve long-stemmed roses, just because you're YOU.
CARED FOR
The breath of a puppy giving kisses as he nips your ears, happy thoughts.
EXPRESSIVE
Birds chirping in the crisp morning air, welcoming a brand-new day; significant.
RESPECTED
The magical sound of a child's laughter; innocence, never violated.

CONTENT
Saying yes to Jesus for the very first time; given peace
as you take a deep breath.
LISTENED TO
A heart to heart with your spouse, given full attention.
ADMIRED
A visit from your kids and grandkids, unconditional love.
LIKE JESUS
Dreaming the most beautiful dream ever about always
forgiving and being forgiven.

The creator of all things, God Himself,
created the most beautiful creation of all, YOU!

As the moon approaches and kisses the sky,
so does your Heavenly Father kiss your cheek,
for you had strayed, but have come home.

HEARTBEAT OF HOPE

MARCH 12, 2016

Our heart . . . What an amazing organ!
With every beat, we live, we breathe, we love,
we feel, we create, we imagine.
Do we ever look at the condition of our heart? WE SHOULD!
Our heart tells the truth! Our heart cannot lie!
God created our hearts so as to rebuild;
to be courageous, to love, not hate!
Our self-centered humanity stepped in.
Believing we had a better way, we created chaos,
instead of peace as God intended!
Our passionate, all-powerful, loving, forgiving God
placed within Gabriel a very special, gracious, and courageous heart.
His heart gave. His heart loved. His heart cared about people.
His heart wanted the best for people. His heart saw the best in people.
You are one of those very special people!
You were blessed to have Gabriel in your life!
The path that Gabriel chose to walk was full of making memories,
making mistakes but learning from them,
choosing friends that could help him along life's journey,
keeping family close and loving them,
bringing laughter and when needed,
giving you the pep talk to keep you going in the right direction.
Create in me a clean heart, O God.
Renew a right spirit within me.
Psalm 51:10
Our heart . . . Such an amazing organ!
What is the condition of your heart/my heart?
Shall we honor Gabriel by doing a heart check?
Shall we love, not hate. Be truthful, not lie.

See the best in people, not the worst.
Be uplifting in our words, not tearing down.
Encourage, not discourage. Be generous, not selfish.
Hold each other up, not pull each other down.
Be happy for another person when they succeed, not jealous.
Love one another as Jesus Christ loves us!
Our hearts deserve a daily check!
In doing so, with every beat, we can continue Gabriel's legacy
by living, breathing, loving, feeling, creating, and imagining!
Our heart . . .
keeping it pure, strong, courageous, and hopeful for the future!

DON'T GIVE UP ON CHRISTMAS

DECEMBER 25, 2015

As I write my annual poem, Christmas is less than two weeks away.
I HAVE ONE REQUEST
DO NOT GIVE UP ON CHRISTMAS!
The true meaning of Christmas!
Everyone with their own take on Christmas. It's gonna happen!
Can I ask you politely to hear mine?
With the atmosphere so grand!
The kindness, the giving, more contagious, more prominent!
Shoppers, packages, traffic out in full force.
Hidden deep within, the parade of loneliness, sadness,
the missing of loved ones resides.
Smiles, genuine or masked, still beautiful.
Hearts still empty. Hearts stay empty without the
"True Meaning of Christmas."
Jesus, the babe, born in the most humble way on that Silent Night.
Be honest, look deep within. No more hiding. No more pretending.
Ask yourself: What is true happiness? When all is going well?
Relationships, family, health, job, money, on and on . . .
Be honest, look deep within. Ask yourself:
How can I have true happiness?
Every day something; my life in chaos!
Was it a choice I made or not? Does it really matter? It's reality right?
I'm just like you. I struggle with all that too!
I JUST DON'T WEAR MY MASK ANYMORE!
I say #keepitreal #keepitsimple
Jesus helps me do that! He keeps me sane seriously!
Stay calm. He's got this! I tell myself that.
All the philosophies, beliefs, or unbeliefs, the facts,
the truth cannot be changed!

I've experienced Him in my life! Hard times, happy times;
that babe in a manger is for real!
HE NEVER GAVE UP ON ME
I would walk away, He stayed true!
Jesus is the "True Meaning of Christmas."
It is the Christmas Season. A time for reflection, a time for emotion.
I ask you to take your mask off. I ask you to not give up on Christmas!

WHERE ARE YOU?

MAY 2010

I call out, but you're not there. Why?
Where are you when I need you?
I feel like I'm all alone. No one knows; it's my secret.
I feel like I have to look good on the outside,
when on the inside, my heart is aching.
I think it's all good when I'm doin' it
You know, making all the bad choices.
Then that haunting feeling again.
I've tried many times to live for you.
My heart so at peace when I was with you.
Why do I let the cares of this life pull me away?
Why when I try, I fail? Listen to my heart; Help me!

You are not a failure to me!
The path you are on will lead you to me.
Choose to live for me again.
I designed you to be hooked up with me,
to go through this life together. I am here.
You keep trying everything else but Me to fill that emptiness.
Only I can fill your emptiness with My love,
peace, joy, and contentment.
I will heal your broken heart.
Isn't this what you really long for?
My heart is breaking as I watch you,
when I have so much for you. Come to me!
The search can be over; come back to me.
I long to hear your voice talk to me.
I long for you to open my book and
read the beautiful plans I have for you.

Don't you see? I am all you need!
Come back to me; we will walk this life together always.
I will always be here. Call out to me; I will come running.
I love you more than you know! Don't run from me any longer.
I will fill your empty heart! Others have failed you;
you trusted them and they failed you. They lead you away from me
and you followed. Don't follow them any longer! Follow me!
I will never fail you! You can trust me!
I will always be with you, through the sunrises and sunsets.
I made them; they are mine. I made you; you are mine.

I call out, but you're not there. Why? Where are you when I need you?
Please listen to my heart. Help me!

I am here with you. You are so precious to me.
We are together now, walking through this life.
You are mine and I am yours. You are okay now.
Not only do you look good on the outside,
but I have healed your broken heart.
You called out to me and I came running.
I love you; we are now together, forever!

I CHERISH YOU, MY SON

MAY 1, 2010

Out of the deepest part of me, I created you.
Did you know that when I created you,
I put inside of you unique qualities
that no other human being has?
When I look at you, I smile.
When I look at you, my heart
can hardly contain
the love I have for you.
When I gently touch you
in the middle of the night
while you are sleeping,
tears of joy stream down my face.
You exist because I needed you to exist.
I put inside of you great qualities,
like no other.
I love how I made you!
You are filled with so much worth.
Your heart is genuine.
You are fun to be with; I love being with you!
How about that imagination of yours;
you turn it into a reality!
I have to compliment myself;
I think I did a great job with your looks too!
I couldn't choose just anyone to place in the
role I have placed you in.
I needed this person to choose to live for me.
To choose to invite my son into his heart.
To choose to live a life that would glorify me.
To be an example to this culture
that has turned against me.

You did this! You chose to live for me!
You humbled your heart and said yes;
I will do this for you, Father.
I dance over you, son, with such love, pride, and joy.
I BELIEVE IN YOU!
Do you see? I need you!
I want to take you to places you've never dreamed of.
I want you to touch lives that no one else can.
In me and through me, you will weather every storm.
You have the heart of a warrior.
You are my warrior, son.
Take me with you everywhere you go.
Son, I love you more than you know. You make me smile.
Out of the deepest part of me, I created you.
I created you in such a unique, special way.
Son, thank you for loving me back. I need your love.
I'm so excited for the day when we will see each other.
My very special son, together forever with me.
Thank you for loving me, for your commitment.
You are my most prized possession.
You are forever in my heart!

THE ONLY ONE

JUNE 19, 2011

The roles you must fill are many. You know it
takes a very unique and special man! How do you do it?
I have to imagine that at times the feeling must be overwhelming;
the pressure, the stress.
Sometimes, your role must leave you feeling like this
is absolutely impossible!
But if anyone can do it, YOU CAN!
You are so strong! I look at you in amazement!
I look at you sometimes and feel ashamed. Ashamed because I've
mistreated you, not giving you the time and respect you deserve.
You work hard! In your eyes, I see disappointment,
discouragement. You feel like what you do is not enough.
Believe that it is quite the opposite! ONLY YOU can fill, and may
I say, fill quite handsomely, all the different roles!
Husband, Father, Grandpa, Provider, Mechanic, Handyman, etc.
Think about this, the times you wonder what you did wrong
when you were only trying to help and do your best?
I'M SORRY!
You are respected, appreciated, beautiful, honored, important,
significant, valued, and loved by your family; created by God!
You are very unique and special!
You are "THE ONLY ONE" who can fill your shoes and you
do it with love and strength! THANK YOU!

EASTER-JESUS-YOU

APRIL 5, 2015

The days are young, but for how long?
In a blink of an eye, some of us will be gone!
Just turn on the news. Our world is full of anxiety and fear!
Do you wonder as I, can it be? Are my prayers being heard?
The reassurance that they are,
brings an overwhelming sense of hope deep inside!
Let me explain: If you believe nothing else, BELIEVE THIS!
Easter is in Webster as follows:
A church feast observed on a Sunday in March or April
in commemoration of Christ's resurrection.
The Gospel News, The Good News
The hope and peace we can live in every day through Jesus Christ!
Easter represents Jesus! He is The Good News!
WE NEED SOME GOOD NEWS!
The Easter story, You are a part of it!
I'm living proof; IT'S TRUE!
As I live each day, each individual I encounter,
is as unique as every sunrise!
You were created to thrive, not just survive!
To live in peace; with hope deep inside.
IMAGINE IT, DREAM IT, SPEAK IT, LIVE IT! YOU CAN!
THE EASTER STORY
THE GOOD NEWS
JESUS CHRIST
HE LIVES to walk with you all the days of your life!
Your days are young, but for how long?
In a blink of an eye, some of us will be gone!
If you believe nothing else, BELIEVE THIS!
THE EASTER STORY—YOU ARE IN IT!

SEARCH NO MORE

OCTOBER 4, 2015

How did I get to this place?
Out of the despair in my heart, I cried.
I wanted to walk out of the darkness.
I wanted to, but it seemed as though I was being held.
Held by my own emotions of not wanting to let go.
Not wanting to let go of the circumstance that brought me to this place.
If I held on, maybe you'd still be here; I could go on.
I felt as if I was sinking. Being swallowed by my heartache of loss.
Suddenly I felt the atmosphere change.
I had an overwhelming sense of strength.
This kind of strength, one I didn't recognize.
How could this happen?
I wasn't asking; I didn't know how.
BUT—LOVE CAME DOWN
this kind of love, so overwhelmingly powerful.
So genuine and true!
At that moment, I knew I could go on! I knew I wanted to live on!
I knew in that instant, my life has a purpose.
My life has meaning.
My life is meant to be, not taken!
My life is meant to overflow into another life that needs me.
An abundance of tears streaming down my face,
once filled with sorrow, hopelessness, and fear.
Now those same tears filled with
joy, hope, and faith.
The God who created me is with me, loving me in my darkest hour.
In my darkest hour, I received His love.
In His love, I've experienced peace.
With His love, I need nothing else.
I SEARCH NO MORE

TO YOU, MY HEART'S STORY

DECEMBER 25, 2012

From the very deepest part of me, my pen
will try to articulate my heart's story.
The day is dawning; a brand-new day.
What will I do with it?
How I look at life, my life,
has changed over the years.
So many choices I have,
as I have been given another new day.
A new day to breathe, to give, to love,
to be thankful. I am thankful!
My family is beautiful to me.
My circle of friends, I treasure.
Those that my precious Jesus
has purposely put in my path,
I am blessed to know,
for I have learned from them.
From the very deepest part of me, my pen
is trying to tell my heart's story.
My heart is heavy for the lost.
I was once lost. Jesus had people praying for me.
Jesus was praying for me, as He is for you.
I was once hopeless, wanting to end it all.
That is so sad to me now.
I pray for all the lost and hopeless people in this world.
That is what is most important to me.
I don't care what you've done; I pray for you.
I once was lost, but now I am found.
Thank You, my Heavenly Father, for sending

Jesus, your only son, as a babe in a manger,
so that I could have hope again.
So that I can pray for those who feel like I used to.
From the very deepest part of me, my pen
has only articulated a very small piece of my heart's story.
Even as I put my pen down, I am praying for you.
The Good News at this beautiful season is Jesus Christ.
He came in such a humble way to save us.
Today as I awake, I ask myself,
"What will I do with this day I have been given?"
I pray that I will first say thank you to my Savior,
Jesus Christ, for never leaving me. For being so kind to me.
For pouring out His grace, His mercy, His love upon my life.
Then in return, I pray He will help me do the same for you.

WHAT WOULD THEY SAY?

JUNE 17, 2012

What will they say as they wash their tears away?
Will they be tears of joy or tears of pain?
Happy tears or tears from a broken heart?
Memories of days gone by that will forever stay in their minds.

My home is a safe place for my heart to be heard.
Maybe my day was crummy and I was feeling down.
Maybe I was excited and had to just let it fly!
How wonderful to know that either way I knew I was safe.
I felt secure. I was understood. I could be myself!

As I walked into the unknown full of anxiety and fear;
my heart pounding not knowing what to expect.
I stayed away as long as I could,
but the time came, I had to face him.
As I entered, there came the word
that carved another piece out of my heart.
Then the ugly stare that made me feel all alone;
or was it the silence that made me feel like I didn't exist?
Always hoping this time it wouldn't be the sound
of a beating whip against my bare skin, never knowing why.

I'm just a child; it's not my fault!
Why do you yell at me just because I asked a question
or expressed my feelings?
Life is a journey. All of us, every day, are learning together!
We can learn from each other, no matter what age we are.
We can talk! I have ideas too!
If you've made mistakes, believe me, IT'S NEVER TOO LATE!

SAY I AM SORRY!
If you think you can do this alone,
throw down that stinkin' pride; become God's own!
We need you they say. Love me in your own special way!
Put down the remote; spend some time with me.
Teach me how to survive in this world, God's way!
My heart needs ALL OF YOU!

Suddenly, I woke up; my heart pounding, tears in my eyes.
Oh, how I need to make things right before it's too late!
God in His love, gave me a wake-up call!
I had been looking back at different scenes of my life;
closing in on the conclusion of my own funeral.
I am so thankful that there is a merciful God,
that when we ask, He puts us all back together again!
As I closed my eyes again,
I could see all of my children, my beautiful grandchildren.
I WONDERED, WHAT WOULD THEY SAY? You have ONE
chance! Let your children/grandchildren
see Jesus Christ, the Potter,
make something beautiful out of YOU!

YOUR JOURNEY, GOD'S PLAN

NOVEMBER 25, 2016

When we look back at our lives, what do we see?
What do you see?
I guess it may depend on our perspective!
Perspective is critical; it can be positive or negative!
It can bring us happiness or sadness!
Your journey has been your own. God is always involved!
You choose, He goes with it always having the bigger plan!
Through times of adversity and struggle, He is with you!
As you journey, making decisions at times, not the best, He is there.
He is there, watching, protecting, speaking, holding you.
He orchestrates, always wanting the best for you.
Your own unique journey has a purpose,
a reason for all that you've overcome.
Now, He will use you to help others! To help others overcome!
You see, you have stumbled, struggled, gone through
hard times for an eternal purpose!
These times have built in you a strong, compassionate character!
You were created for such a time as this!
You will now step into another's hardship,
struggle, sadness and tears.
You will carry them as Jesus carried you; He will help you to do so!
You will give hope to another as God has given you hope!
Take this to heart as it is a precious gift from heaven!
Give from the love you have been given.
God's love will shine through you to this broken world!
God has put His angels in charge over you
to keep you in all your ways!
You chose, God went with you!
He always had the bigger plan!

For I know the thoughts and plans that I have for you,
says the Lord,
thoughts and plans for welfare and peace
and not for evil, to give you hope in your final outcome.
Jeremiah 29:11, NLV

JESUS CAME

DECEMBER 25, 2011

He came for me, how sweet the story.
He came for me in all His glory.
My human mind cannot comprehend,
so He gave me faith to understand.
My heart cries out; it won't lie. My heart cries out;
it can't deny the love I feel deep inside.
He came to catch every tear, soothe every pain;
wait with me in the dark, quiet, lonely place.
This old world tries to push him away. I won't let them,
I need him with me every day!
He is my heart's desire; I long only for him!
Jesus Christ, lover of my soul.
The Only One who has made me whole.
The Only One who loves me as I am;
who gave me a second chance. My life is in your hands!
On that cool December night, all the stars shining so bright;
whether you believe it or not,
it's true, He came for you! To save your soul. To make you whole.
He'll catch all your tears, soothe your pain.
He'll wait with you in your dark, quiet, lonely place.
When no one else knows what you're going through,
He does; He's there for you!
His name is Jesus Christ-The Son of God.
He is my Savior, Redeemer, King.
He is my Hope when it seems as though there is none.
He is my Protector, my Refuge when I am afraid.
He is my Strength when I have nothing left.
It's Christmas time again. The atmosphere has changed.
May our hearts be tender. May our minds be renewed
with the hope of a Savior, Jesus Christ.

He arrived on the scene, so tiny, so humble.
To capture our hearts, yours and mine. To save us!
The Christ of Christmas (maybe think of him as that tiny,
innocent baby boy) is waiting.
Waiting to hear you say YES! YES, my heart invites you in!
YES, I want my life in your hands!
I cry out, Oh Lord, I believe, but please, help my unbelief!
Do you feel the release? Your insides have never felt such peace!
Listen to your heart, it is now tender for real.
Don't be afraid to express what it desperately feels!
It's Christmas time again! The atmosphere has amazingly changed!
So hear this reminder that comes straight from my heart;
look into my eyes and see the truth.
Always remember; don't you ever forget, He came for you!
He'll heal your heart. He'll make you new.
JESUS CAME, HE CAME JUST FOR YOU!

For God so greatly loved and dearly prized the world that he gave up
His only begotten (unique) Son, so that whoever believes in (trusts
in, clings to, relies on) Him shall not perish (come to destruction, be
lost), but have eternal (everlasting) life.
For God did not send His Son into the world in order to judge (to
reject, to condemn, to pass sentence on) the world, but that the world
might find salvation and be made safe and sound through Him.
John 3:16–17

As I pray for you, I ask Jesus to make this Christmas a very special
one in every way!

FOR YOU, FOR ME

MARCH 31, 2013

Love, hung on a cross.
Arms stretched out, hands open.
No holding back for you and for me.
Is that what love is?
No holding back? Giving it all?
No matter what the response
from the one you are showing love to?
Is that called unconditional love?
Wow, that must be hard!
Not for Jesus,
for the love of the Father was flowing through him.
The love of the Father was overtaking all fear,
all anxiousness, all pain.
The love of the Father spoke out and said,
"Please do this. I love them.
My son, I love you, but this is the only way."
He did. He chose to hang on that cross.
He went through it,
knowing after it was all said and done;
knowing that after he was made fun of, spit on,
bullied, dragged, beaten unrecognizable,
carrying his own death sentence,
enduring excruciating pain that you and I
will never have to bear, because He did.
He did this unselfishly for you and I.
He did this because of love.
He did this for the love between him and his Father.
He did this so that you and I,
IF we "CHOOSE" to believe in Him,
IF we "CHOOSE" we will have life, even after we die

WITH HIM FOREVER!
This is beyond comprehension!
Don't do that to yourself; make yourself all crazy!
You'll make yourself all crazy trying to figure it out!
YOU CAN'T! HAVE FAITH!
Faith in "The One" who loves YOU!
JESUS hung on the cross, the cross that expresses forgiveness.
With His arms stretched out with love.
With His hands open, showing surrender.
FOR YOU, FOR ME!

I'M GLAD YOU'RE MINE

THANKSGIVING DAY
NOVEMBER 27, 2014

When I think about family,
I think of you!
How would my life be
different without you?
I suppose if I'd never known you,
I'd be fine.
Knowing you, though, now has given me
an outlook on life
that I never want to not have!
You are a part of me!
You own a piece of my heart!
When I think of you, I am proud; I smile!
I thank Jesus every day
for making you a part of me, my life!
When I see you, it's like a flower opening;
it's purpose revealed.
When it closes, our time together has to end,
yet it leaves a shadow
which follows me; always with me.
When I think of family,
I think of you, my family!
The family that was given to me
as a gift from our Heavenly Father.
I treasure my gift! I cherish my gift!
I am so thankful for my gift, YOU!
I LOVE YOU!
I'm Glad You're Mine!

MIRROR ME

JUNE 15, 2014

What kind of a Father are you?

The Bible says,

Fathers, do not provoke your children to anger by the way you treat them. Rather, bring them up with the discipline and instruction that comes from the Lord.

Ephesians 6:4

In the midst of a world with people, young and old;

full of anger, immorality, indifferences, hate, mind altering substances, hurt, insecurities and ugly prideful egos.

LOOK AROUND! Why do you think it's so bad?

Our world has said NO to God! Can't do that!

The worst decision we could ever make!

From the moment a child is born, you are teaching them.

They watch you; they listen to you. What did you just do? What did you just say? I didn't know that was wrong to do or say? I saw you do it! I heard you say that!

I'M YOU, just little!

PATIENCE: Explain the whys and why nots.

LISTEN: to them without interrupting.

Give hugs, say I'm sorry, move on!

We need Dads who stand up for what is right!

We need Dads who are strong and speak out for justice!

IS THAT YOU? CAN YOU SAY, MIRROR ME?

The Bible says,

Fathers, do not aggravate your children,

or they will become discouraged.

Colossians 3:21

Your children are beautiful, valuable treasures.

Guard them, protect their innocence, repair any broken words or actions, forgive, impart goodness into their lives.
Say I'M SORRY, FORGIVE AGAIN!
A Father is a leader; a world changer;
teach your children to be the same!
WE NEED YOU, DADS AND GRANDPAS!
WE LOVE OUR DADS AND GRANDPAS!
At times asking ourselves the hard questions is good!
What kind of a Father am I?
Can you say to your children, MIRROR ME?

THE HOPE CHEST

DECEMBER 25, 2009

The anticipation! I can hardly stand it!
Waiting for something good to happen.
Filling your hope chest with the anticipation of a birthday,
a new born baby, a sporting event, a vacation,
shopping, the visitation of a family member or friend,
a new car, a new house, a new job, an adventure,
and possibly the birth of a Savior?
What a great emotion anticipation brings.
It brings excitement, hope, wonder, warm fuzzies,
maybe even past wonderful memories.
With all of this said and as wonderful as it all may be,
the greatest anticipation of all time must have been
the birth of our Savior, Jesus Christ.
All these other things are temporary fulfillments,
always wanting another anticipation
to put in my hope chest.
But the anticipation of a Savior,
the hope He brings in our hearts,
will last forever and never get old.
We'll never need a replacement or have another want.
The hope that Jesus can bring to a heart
is the most exciting anticipation of all time.
This Christmas, maybe for the first time,
you will start filling your hope chest
with things you have been missing
in your heart for a long time. And when your hope chest is full of all
the missing parts,
Then Jesus comes to fulfill all the longings
of your heart and your
Hope Chest is complete in Him.

HER JOURNEY, HER STORY

I Call Her "Baby Girl"
April 9, 2016

Life is a journey. Everyone has a story to tell!
This is a very special one!
This one is about "Baby Girl"!
You dreamed about her for so long.
Tears became a way of life; hopes shattered.
Giving life is worth fighting for!
Never giving up; never giving in to fear, heartache, or being let down.
You had to be brave. You had to have courage.
You had to push forward.
With love, hope, and faith leading the way!
The tenderness of grace touched you deep within your souls!
Miracles cannot be explained. They are to be treasured!
Their purpose is to help you believe!
They are a gift from God!
TIMING IS EVERYTHING!
God's timing is always perfect! To trust and wait builds faith!
I've always called her "Baby Girl"!
I've kept her covered with prayer!
The life she will lead, the lives she will touch
will be graced with the genuineness of her heart,
the honesty of her character, the pureness of her love!
LIFE IS A JOURNEY!
Her journey began with courage, love, hope, and faith!
Two lives giving life to their baby girl.
This special life has a very special story to tell!
THIS ONE BELONGS TO "BABY GIRL"!

MY HAND, YOUR NAME

JULY 17, 2010
FROM THE HEART OF JESUS

Have you ever thought about what the definition of "CHOSEN" is?
CHOSEN: Picked out by preference. Selected. Elect.
Chosen by God for salvation and eternal life.
That is amazing! Think about it: YOU ARE "CHOSEN"!
Chosen by God, the maker of heaven and earth.
The One who knows everything about you.
The One who loves you unconditionally.
Understand this: Jesus says to you:
I CHOSE YOU!
Jesus created you just the way you are for His purposes.
Your specific qualities are meant to touch lives.
No one else is like you!
Jesus needs you to touch souls that He puts in your path.
He wants them to live in victory like He has destined for you to.
No more living in your past. It's over and today is a new day!
Jesus says this to you:
Devote much of your time to spend with me!
I so long for that! I want to give you My character.
Spend time with me. Let Me change you like only I can.
I need to be your focus. I need to be your priority.
I am your lifeline. Open up My Word of Life and absorb it all!
Live by MY WORD! Don't let anyone or anything
have your attention!
I love you; I made you very special!
The words on this page are from My heart.
Your heart is the one I want!
You are My "Chosen One." You are going to touch so many lives.
You are a Beacon of Light for Me!

Answer your call. Don't wait! This is your time.
Say yes and know I am with you. Don't live in your past any longer!
Concentrate on Me; make Me first in your life.
No regrets anymore; stop worrying about things
that you cannot control.
I am in control of everything!
Let me lead you; let me guide you; let me direct you. Trust Me!
I love you; I picked you out; I selected you.
Once and for all, commit your life to Me
and let's walk this road together.
When you decide to say yes, I will be so happy!
You see, I will never force you.
I don't want you to be hurt or sad any longer! I will help you.
Come to Me; decide now!
I have chosen you to live for Me and for us to walk
out this life together.
CHOSEN: Picked out by preference. Selected. Elect.
Chosen by God for salvation and eternal life.
When Jesus defined "CHOSEN," He did so by writing
"Your Name" on the palm of His hand.

JESUS, THE DARLING
OF HEAVEN

DECEMBER 25, 2016

The Christmas story
What does it mean to me; to you? What has it done in me; in you?
Have you ever taken the time; quiet, uninterrupted time,
to think about the story?
To read it again or read it for the very first time! (Luke 2)
This is Christ's beginning on earth, the darling baby Jesus!
He is real you know! The darling of heaven, God's son!
What a road He traveled!
We don't think of it much now do we? Do we care??
I mean with our busy lifestyles, our schedules,
all we have to fit into our day.
How is it possible? Possible to add one more thing?
What's important to me, to you?
Our families, friends, jobs, homes, education,
bucket list, cell phones, social lives?
JESUS? Where does He fit in?
Summer rains, delightful cuisine, breathtaking sunsets,
laughter, memorable moments,
peace in the valley, comfort in the storm, miraculous provision,
joy-filled rewards,
tears of heartache become treasures in our hearts . . . gifts from heaven!
JESUS? Where does He fit in? Right here! Right now!
Right in the midst of life!
Life is tough at times! Life can be hard at times! We all go through it!
Life is beautiful, amazing, wonderful, exciting!
The road Jesus traveled, He traveled for me, for you! Do we care?
His road was full of hardship, sacrifice, miracles, and love!
Do we care? We need to!

Can Jesus fit into your busy life? He can if you invite him to fit!
He will fit like that last puzzle piece that will make your life complete!
Will you consider taking the time; quiet, uninterrupted time,
to think about the story?
To read it again, or read it for the very first time! (Luke 2) I did!
What's important to me; to you?
What has the story done in me; in you?
Have you allowed His story to change you? I have!
Have you allowed His story to heal your broken, hurting,
unforgiving, lonely heart? I have!
Jesus was that puzzle piece I needed to make my life complete!
He is real you know! The darling of heaven, God's son!
Jesus Christ is Christmas!

A MANGER, A CROSS

TWO JOURNEYS
DECEMBER 25, 2013

What journey are you on?
From the time we are conceived, we are on a journey!
A very unique journey! A journey made up of decisions and choices.
These decisions and choices could be made
by another person or yourself.
Where have you come from?
Where are you going on your journey?
This is your life, your one opportunity!
Would you like to change your direction? It's NEVER too late!
Mary, the mother of Jesus had a choice.
She could have said NO to the angel that appeared to her,
for she was the one whom God chose to bear the Christ Child.
HARD CHOICES TAKE COURAGE and FAITH!
In doing so, the outcome brings triumph to those
who believe why the hard choices had to be made!
The journey was long,
but Mary persevered and our Savior was born!
The manger scene; how can it not touch your heart?
For it is there that Jesus begins another journey.
The journey to The Cross!
You know that's why He had to be born right?
Gods plan to save His creation from perishing.
God loved us so much that He made a way for us to be saved
through His Son, Jesus Christ!
Why wouldn't you accept His free gift?
Jesus is our bridge to our Heavenly Father.
He filled in the gap for us. He is the ONLY WAY
we can be one with our Creator!

THERE IS NO GREATER LOVE THAN THIS!
Jesus said yes! YES, I will go to The Cross!
HARD CHOICES TAKE COURAGE and FAITH!
The outcome though, brings triumph to those
who believe why the hard choices had to be made!
TWO JOURNEYS
Both not only took perseverence, but a deep love for all mankind!
Stemming down from God,
Mary knew she had to make the right choice.
When she did, God's plan and purpose could be fulfilled!
HER JOURNEY—THE MANGER
Jesus, knowing what He was going to have to endure, said YES,
I choose to do the right thing!
HIS JOURNEY—THE CROSS
What will you choose to do with your journey?
Your Heavenly Father loves you this much
that He set both of these journeys into motion for YOU!
He had two willing vessels, Mary and Jesus,
who chose to do the right thing
with courage and faith!
Do you have enough courage and faith
to do the right thing, to make the hard choices?
I BELIEVE YOU DO!
I BELIEVE IN YOU!

ALL ALONG, HE HELD US

01/06/13

Not knowing as my heart was breaking, He was holding me.
You see, sometimes I felt so alone as I was feeling,
"Was I the cause of this lingering outcome?"
Am I to blame as I watched this real life story unfold?
I tried my best to understand and be there.
To be the ear, the hands, the shoulder.
WAS IT NOT ENOUGH?
It was out of my control;
what was happening couldn't be stopped.
It had to come to pass for the greater purpose.
As the story is unfolding,
daily, my chest almost bursting open
with expectation of what will happen next?
One day filled with hope, the next desperation.
Not knowing as my heart was breaking, He was holding me.
I would hold my breath, not wanting to breathe,
but to stay in the moment.
The moment when I felt some hope,
as if the story would have a happy ending.
Looking into his eyes wanting answers,
just give me the truth, the truth that never seemed to come.
I guess it was too hard, trapped in the cave of
deepening sorrow and despair.
The lies, not wanting to cause more hurt,
believing his own lie that he could do it alone.
As the days unfold, not knowing as my heart
continued to break, He was holding me.

How does it happen that somehow, someway, I kept getting up,
going, believing, living, loving him; even though he was why
I felt my heart would burst open at any moment,
not able to close again.
He was holding me through it all; infusing into me
peace, faith and the drive to keep going.
My desperate prayers somehow gave me hope;
the willingness to continue.
As I still live in the uncertainty in my natural mind; at the same time
I live with certainty in my heart that it's going to be fine.
Healing is taking place in me and him.
The days continue to unfold,
some nights longer than others,
but deep down I know Jesus is holding US.

WHY I BELIEVE

APRIL 24, 2011

I guess you could say that I've always been the trusting kind.
I like to think that there's good in everyone.
I'd like to believe that one day we'll all get along and quit fighting.
But is this realistic? YES, because I believe it is!
When you truly believe in something or someone,
you are solid as a rock!
No one can change your mind!
This is how I feel about Jesus Christ!
You may ask, but how did you get to that point in your life?
How did you come to believe?
Are you ever just tired? Tired of the way your life is going?
Tired of the day in and day out drama?
Tired of wondering where you are headed and why you were born?
Tired of faking it on the outside, making everyone
believe you have it all together,
when you are really dying on the inside?
Tired of the emptiness, the void in your heart?
I know that these thoughts and many more
have gone through all of our minds.
Well, this is exactly where I was at, but I didn't know what to do.
I wanted to give up!
My life was too overwhelming to me. Day in and day out LIFE!
Have you ever had something or someone
come to you just at the right time?
Like if it wouldn't have happened or they didn't come,
then you didn't know what you were going to do.
That's it, you said it! It happened; He came; He saved me!
I didn't pray; I didn't ask or make a request.
He just arrived on the scene to rescue me.

In my really dark place, my Hero came. He came
and He picked me up! Jesus embraced me!
I felt His love, such love as I've never felt before!
I immediately trusted and believed!
I didn't have to try and figure it out. I didn't have to ask questions.
I didn't have to have an explanation. I didn't have to get all theological.
I JUST BELIEVED! WHY NOT?
When the person of Jesus Christ comes to you,
picks you up out of your dark place
and loves you, why on earth wouldn't you just believe?
I guess you could say that I'm the trusting kind.
I know it's hard for some. You may have to have all the answers,
explanations, ask the questions, and have a theological discussion.
But when you're hurting; in a lost and dark place
and your heart is empty,
I really believe what you truly need and want is for
someone to just come and pick you up and love you,
just like I needed and wanted!
THAT'S WHAT JESUS DID FOR ME!
This is why I believe in HIM;
My Savior, My Redeemer, My Risen King!
This Easter, put all that trying to figure it out away,
and JUST BELIEVE!

ABOUT THE AUTHOR

In 1999, at the age of forty, Jesus Christ finally captured the heart of Ruthann Bond. She was aware of who Jesus was and knew that he was real but just didn't think she needed him. She wanted to live her own life the way that was pleasing to other people. Ruthann was born in Tacoma, Washington. She grew up in the small town of Healdsburg, California. She graduated from Konawaena Highschool on the Big Island of Hawaii in 1976. Her parents were with the organization Youth with a Mission. She now lives in Tucson, Arizona. Her mom is still living, loving Jesus and life. She lost her dad in 1986 to cancer, but he is in heaven with Jesus so happy. She's married to a very special and supportive husband, whom she met in Tucson. They have been married for thirty years. Life together is an adventure with everyday growing as individuals and growing together. The love they share is filled with lots of humor, much joy and always hope. She has three sisters and two brothers. She has three wonderful children, two daughters, and a son, along with their spouses and ten beautiful grandchildren. Her mother-in-law is more like a mom and is very special to her along with the rest of her in-laws. She has a very large and loving family which include many more uncles, aunts, cousins, nieces, nephews, great-nieces, and great-nephews. She adores her family and would do anything for them. She has a heart for people; she cares about them and the difficulties that they may be going through. You will experience this in her writings. Ruthann has fully given her heart to Jesus and gives him all the glory and all the praise for her life, her family, and this opportunity right here. If you ever need prayer for anything, you must contact her, and she will be right on it. She believes in the power of prayer every day. She is an everyday, roll-up-your-sleeves, living-in-the-real-world kind of person. She is genuine and wants you to live in the destiny that God has for you.

CPSIA information can be obtained
at www.ICGtesting.com
Printed in the USA
FFOW02n1646200518
46771688-48944FF